W9-BQI-027

EXPLORING THE STATES

Vermont

THE GREEN MOUNTAIN STATE

by Emily Schnobrich

BLASTOFF! 5 READERS

BELLWETHER MEDIA · MINNEAPOLIS, MN

Note to Librarians, Teachers, and Parents:

Blastoff! Readers are carefully developed by literacy experts and combine standards-based content with developmentally appropriate text.

Level 1 provides the most support through repetition of high-frequency words, light text, predictable sentence patterns, and strong visual support.

Level 2 offers early readers a bit more challenge through varied simple sentences, increased text load, and less repetition of high-frequency words.

Level 3 advances early-fluent readers toward fluency through increased text and concept load, less reliance on visuals, longer sentences, and more literary language.

Level 4 builds reading stamina by providing more text per page, increased use of punctuation, greater variation in sentence patterns, and increasingly challenging vocabulary.

Level 5 encourages children to move from "learning to read" to "reading to learn" by providing even more text, varied writing styles, and less familiar topics.

Whichever book is right for your reader, Blastoff! Readers are the perfect books to build confidence and encourage a love of reading that will last a lifetime!

This edition first published in 2014 by Bellwether Media, Inc.

No part of this publication may be reproduced in whole or in part without written permission of the publisher. For information regarding permission, write to Bellwether Media, Inc., Attention: Permissions Department, 5357 Penn Avenue South, Minneapolis, MN 55419.

Library of Congress Cataloging-in-Publication Data

Schnobrich, Emily.
 Vermont / by Emily Schnobrich.
   pages cm. – (Blastoff! readers. Exploring the states)
 Includes bibliographical references and index.
 Summary: "Developed by literacy experts for students in grades three through seven, this book introduces young readers to the geography and culture of Vermont"–Provided by publisher.
 ISBN 978-1-62617-045-2 (hardcover : alk. paper)
 1. Vermont–Juvenile literature. I. Title.
 F49.3.S35 2014
 974.3–dc23
                                                                    2013002354

Printed in the United States of America, North Mankato, MN.

Table of Contents

Where Is Vermont?

Vermont is a small northern state that covers 9,617 square miles (24,908 square kilometers) just south of Quebec, Canada. It is one of six states that make up **New England**. This region forms the northeastern corner of the United States. It is known for its colorful, hilly landscapes and long history as part of the nation.

Vermont is the only New England state without a coast. It is bordered by the state of Massachusetts in the south. New York is its western neighbor. The Connecticut River separates Vermont from New Hampshire in the east. The capital of Vermont is Montpelier.

New York

Quebec, Canada

Lake Champlain

Burlington

★ Montpelier

Vermont

N

W   E

S

Rutland

Connecticut River

New Hampshire

Massachusetts

History

The Abenaki and other **Native** Americans lived in Vermont before the United States was a country. The French were the first European settlers in Vermont. Later the British took control of the area. Vermont organized its own government in 1777. After the **Revolutionary War**, it became the fourteenth state. Vermont was one of the first states to outlaw **slavery**.

Abenaki Native Americans

Vermont Timeline!

1609: Samuel de Champlain visits Vermont and claims it as French land.

1763: Britain takes control of Vermont.

1770: Vermont hero Ethan Allen forms a group called the Green Mountain Boys. They fight to keep New Yorkers from taking over their territory.

1775: The American Revolutionary War begins.

1777: Vermont creates its own government.

1783: The Revolutionary War ends. The United States of America is formed.

1791: Vermont becomes the fourteenth state.

1881: Vermont native Chester Arthur becomes the twenty-first U.S. President.

1923: Vermont native Calvin Coolidge becomes the thirtieth U.S. President.

1970: Vermont passes the Environmental Control Law. This law protects the state's land and wildlife.

Samuel de Champlain

Ethan Allen

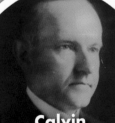

Calvin Coolidge

The Land

Did you know?
Summers in Vermont are mild and rainy. Winters are long and cold with beautiful snow.

Vermont's Climate
average °F

spring
Low: 34°
High: 54°

summer
Low: 58°
High: 78°

fall
Low: 40°
High: 56°

winter
Low: 12°
High: 29°

Most of Vermont's landscape is rolling and rocky. The Taconic Mountains rise up on the state's southwest side. Lowlands line Vermont's eastern border. To the north are the Northeast Highlands. They are marked by granite mountains and flowing rivers. Lakes and ponds also dot the region.

The Champlain Valley lies on Vermont's northwestern border. It is home to the state's largest body of water, Lake Champlain. Vermont's largest city, Burlington, is also located there. The valley has some of the best farmland in the state. Golden fields of wheat and roaming cows are common sights there.

fun fact

Over three-fourths of Vermont is covered in trees. In autumn, Vermonters have festivals to celebrate the brilliant leaves.

The Green Mountains

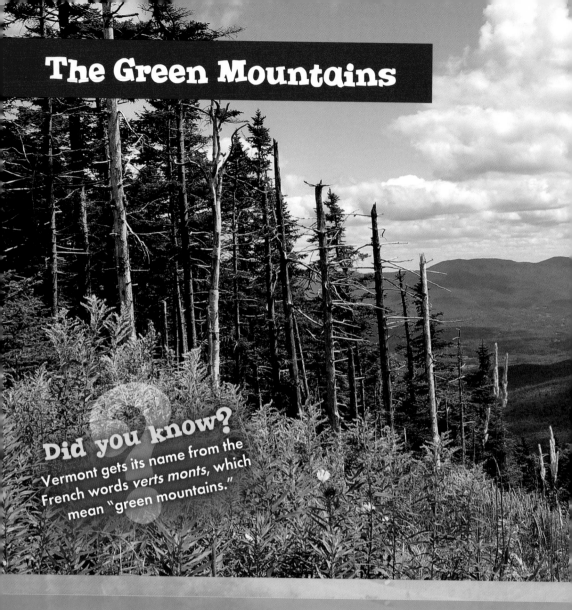

Did you know?
Vermont gets its name from the French words *verts monts*, which mean "green mountains."

The Green Mountains are one of Vermont's most majestic features. They run right down the center of the state like a backbone. The Green Mountains make up the northern part of the Appalachian Mountains. The Appalachians stretch from Canada down to Alabama in the southern United States.

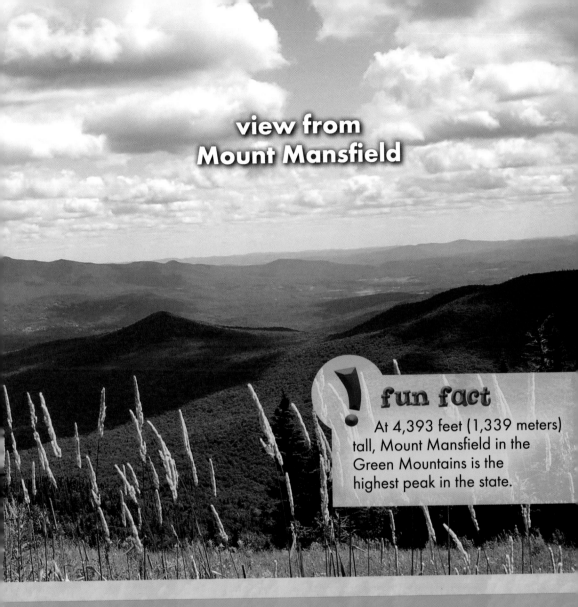

view from
Mount Mansfield

! fun fact

At 4,393 feet (1,339 meters) tall, Mount Mansfield in the Green Mountains is the highest peak in the state.

The Green Mountains are home to many kinds of trees. They are protected by the Green Mountain National Forest. Winter sports fans and **tourists** flock to the mountains. They ski and enjoy the colorful **canopy** that covers the peaks.

Wildlife

A number of furry creatures call Vermont home. The white-tailed deer is one of the most common animals. Moose, bears, and foxes also roam the forests. Beavers build dams in rivers filled with brook trout and walleye. Bald eagles sometimes soar overhead.

Vermont is blanketed with spruces, birches, and other trees. Ferns and wildflowers grow at their feet. Vermont is famous for its state tree, the sugar maple. This tree produces some of the best syrup in the country.

brook trout

white-tailed deer

moose

Canada lynx

fun fact

Canada lynx are wild cats that hunt rabbits in Vermont's forests. They are known for their hairy ears.

Landmarks

Vermont is full of historical landmarks. The Bennington Battle **Monument** celebrates a key battle in the Revolutionary War. It is also the tallest structure in the state. The Old **Constitution** House is another important place. Vermont's first constitution was written there. Visitors to Vermont can also explore Calvin Coolidge's childhood home in Plymouth. He was the thirtieth President of the United States.

Vermont has many granite **quarries**. The Rock of Ages company in Barre gives tours of a quarry that is almost 600 feet (183 meters) deep. White church steeples and covered bridges are other popular sights in the countryside.

Barre quarry

Bennington Battle Monument

Burlington

Burlington is Vermont's largest city. More than 42,000 people live there. The city overlooks the sparkling Lake Champlain. Burlington is home to the University of Vermont. During school months, the city bursts with thousands of energetic students.

Burlington hosts many of Vermont's annual festivals and concerts. Much of the activity takes place downtown at the Church Street Marketplace. This outdoor mall hosts street entertainers and lively events throughout the year. The Burlington Winter Festival is especially popular. A dance party breaks out on the brick street as Vermonters celebrate the winter season.

Church Street
Marketplace

Working

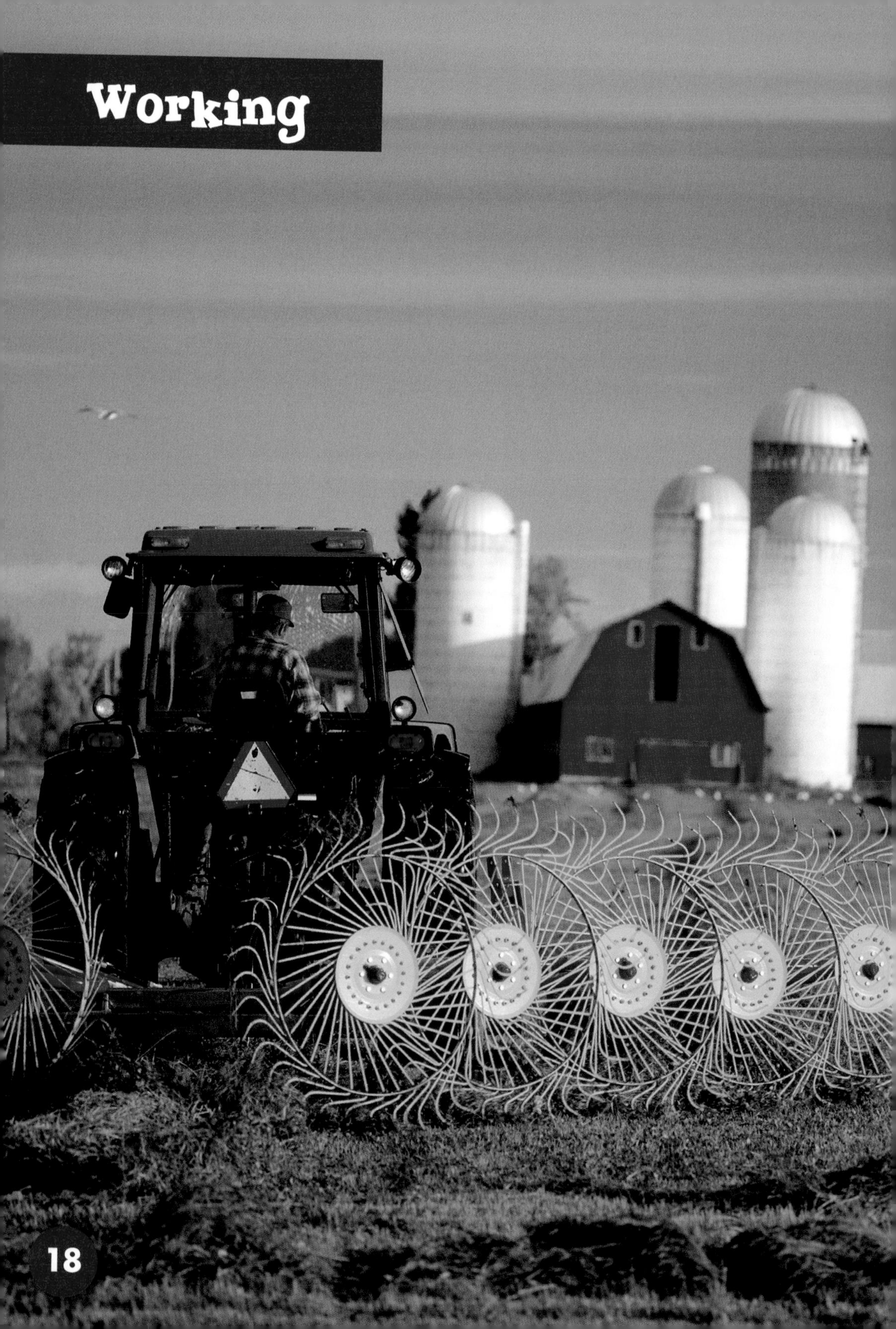

Farmers in Vermont raise cattle for beef and dairy products. They also grow wheat, apples, corn, and potatoes. Some Vermonters make wood and paper products from nearby forests. Others make a living by printing newspapers and books. Many Vermonters make electronics and computer machinery. Some mine for **natural resources** such as granite and marble.

Millions of people travel to Vermont every year. Many Vermonters work **service jobs** to help these tourists at hotels and restaurants. Others run museums, festivals, or their own specialty shops.

Where People Work in Vermont

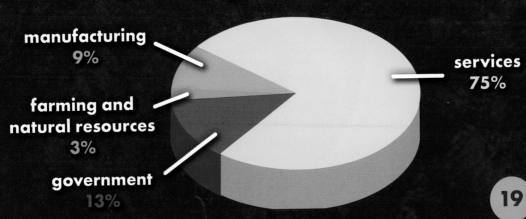

manufacturing
9%

services
75%

farming and
natural resources
3%

government
13%

Playing

Vermont's mountains and open spaces make it the perfect place for outdoor fun. Vermonters like to ice fish, ski, and snowboard during the state's snowy winters. Hiking, camping, and bicycling are also popular activities.

Vermont has always attracted artists and musicians. They enjoy the state's excellent theater and music. They look forward to outdoor concerts and plays during the summer. Vermonters also spend their free time at museums and art fairs.

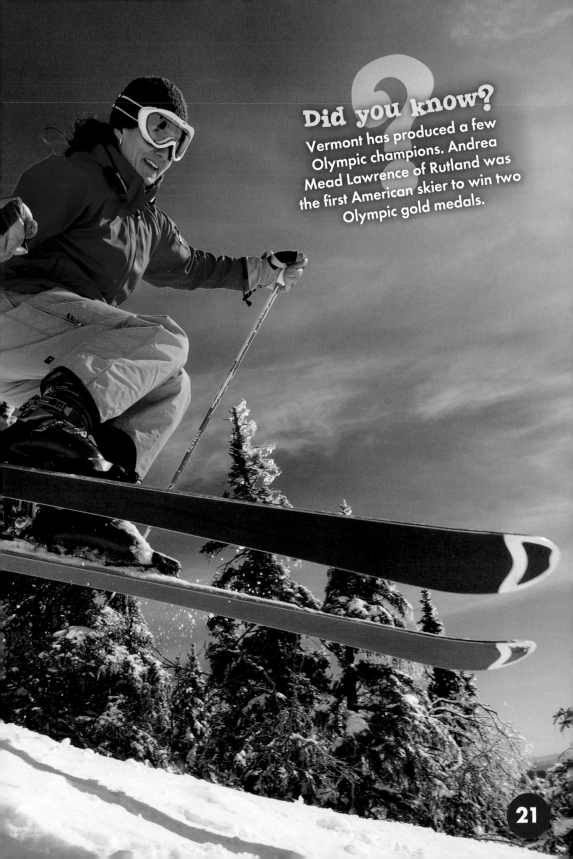

Did you know?

Vermont has produced a few Olympic champions. Andrea Mead Lawrence of Rutland was the first American skier to win two Olympic gold medals.

Apple Muffins

Ingredients:

2 cups white or whole-wheat flour
3/4 cup white sugar
1 tbsp. baking powder
1/4 tsp. baking soda
1 tsp. cinnamon
1/4 tsp. nutmeg
1/2 tsp. salt
1/2 cup milk
1/3 cup oil
2 eggs
1 1/2 cups peeled, diced apples
1/2 cup walnuts

Topping:
1/4 cup sugar and cinnamon, mixed

Directions:

1. Combine all dry ingredients in large bowl and mix well.

2. Combine milk, oil, and eggs in another bowl and mix well.

3. Add liquids to dry ingredients. Add apples and nuts.

4. Line or grease muffin tins and fill 1/4 full with batter. Sprinkle with topping.

5. Bake at 425°F for 20 minutes. Brush with melted butter. Serve warm.

Did you know?
The process of making maple syrup is called sugaring.

fun fact

Ben & Jerry's ice cream company began in Vermont. In 1978, Ben Cohen and Jerry Greenfield started selling their goofy flavors from an old gas station in Burlington.

Vermont is not only known for maple syrup. It is also famous for its dairy products, especially cheese. One of Vermont's biggest cheese producers is Cabot Creamery. Their cheddar is sold in grocery stores across the country. Vermont also produces the most milk of any state in New England.

Many restaurants in Vermont serve local foods. This means that chefs try to use ingredients found in their own community. Apples, honey, potatoes, and corn are common. Hunters and fishers provide rabbit, deer, and walleye.

Festivals

Vermonters are proud of their farming history. They celebrate with events like the Dairy Festival in late spring and the Sheep and Wool Festival in the fall. The Vermont Cheesemakers Festival began in 2009. Hungry visitors can taste cheese and learn how it is made. Every spring in St. Albans, Vermonters gather at the Maple Festival to learn about sugaring. Some people even compete in maple syrup cooking competitions.

In summer, Vermont hosts music festivals and concerts throughout the state. A popular one is the Discover Jazz Festival. Audiences listen to different kinds of jazz and meet the musicians. Theater and opera festivals are other exciting events.

fun fact

The Bread and Puppet Theater participates in festivals across the state. Its giant puppets perform in shows and parades.

Bread and Puppet Theater

Did you know?

Summer in Vermont also brings hot air balloon festivals. Colorful balloons dot the skies as they glide above the Vermont countryside.

The Shelburne Museum

schoolhouse

meeting house

Vermont's Shelburne Museum is located south of Burlington. Nearly 40 buildings make up the museum. Several are art galleries. Inside are colorful American paintings and furniture from as early as the 1600s. Visitors can also explore New England buildings from the 1700s and 1800s. A one-room schoolhouse, **blacksmith** shop, and general store offer a glimpse into early American life.

Ticonderoga

Another major feature of the museum is the 220-foot (67-meter) _Ticonderoga_. Built in 1906, this **steamboat** carried Vermonters across Lake Champlain to New York. Vermont's history and natural beauty truly come to life at the Shelburne Museum.

Fast Facts About Vermont

Vermont's Flag

Vermont's flag is deep blue. In the center, a pine tree, wheat, and a grazing cow stand before mountains. Above this scene is the head of a deer. Below are pine branches and a red banner with the state's name and motto. This version of the flag was adopted in 1923.

State Flower
red clover

State Nickname:	The Green Mountain State
State Motto:	"Freedom and Unity"
Year of Statehood:	1791
Capital City:	Montpelier
Other Major Cities:	Burlington, Rutland
Population:	625,741 (2010)
Area:	9,617 square miles (24,908 square kilometers); Vermont is the 45th largest state.
Major Industries:	tourism, mining, manufacturing, farming
Natural Resources:	granite, marble, limestone, lumber
State Government:	150 representatives; 30 senators
Federal Government:	1 representative; 2 senators
Electoral Votes:	3

State Animal
Morgan horse

State Bird
hermit thrush

29

Glossary

blacksmith—a person who makes tools and other objects out of metal

canopy—a thick covering of leafy branches formed by the tops of trees

constitution—a statement of principles and laws of a city, state, or country

monument—a structure that is built to remember important events or people

native—originally from a specific place

natural resources—materials in the earth that are taken out and used to make products or fuel

New England—a group of six states that make up the northeastern corner of the United States

quarries—large open pits from which rock and other materials are dug

Revolutionary War—the war between 1775 and 1783 in which the United States fought for independence from Great Britain

service jobs—jobs that perform tasks for people or businesses

slavery—a system in which certain people are considered property

steamboat—a boat or ship that is powered by steam

tourists—people who travel to visit another place

To Learn More

AT THE LIBRARY

Alvarez, Julia. *Return to Sender.* New York, N.Y.:
Alfred A. Knopf, 2009.

Blegvad, Lenore. *Kitty and Mr. Kipling: Neighbors
in Vermont.* New York, N.Y.: Margaret K. McElderry
Books, 2005.

Czech, Jan M. *Vermont.* New York, N.Y.: Children's
Press, 2009.

ON THE WEB

Learning more about Vermont
is as easy as 1, 2, 3.

1. Go to www.factsurfer.com.

2. Enter "Vermont" into the search box.

3. Click the "Surf" button and you will see a list of
   related Web sites.

With factsurfer.com, finding more information is just
a click away.

Index

The images in this book are reproduced through the courtesy of: Brian Jannsen/ Age Fotostock/
SuperStock, front cover (bottom); Hugh Manatee/ Wikipedia, p. 6; (Collection)/ Prints & Photographs
Division/ Library of Congress, p. 7 (left & right); Getty Images, p. 7 (middle); John Churchman/
Corbis/ Glow Images, pp. 8-9; Jay Boucher, pp. 10-11; Jurgen & Christine Sohns/ FLPA/ Glow
Images, pp. 12-13; James Marvin Phelps, p. 12 (left); Richard Seeley, p. 12 (middle); Dec Hogan,
p. 12 (right); Vicki Beaver/ Alamy, p. 14; Andre Jenny Stock Connection Worldwide/ Newscom,
pp. 14-15; Stefan Auth/ Glow Images, pp. 16-17; George Robinson Stock Connection Worldwide/
Newscom, p. 18; Yellow Dog Productions/ Getty Images, p. 19; SuperStock/ Glow Images,
p. 20; SuperStock/ Age Fotostock, pp. 20-21; Charles Brutlag, p. 22; Randy M. Ury/ Corbis/
Glow Images, p. 23; Jon Eppard, p. 23 (right); Age Fotostock, p. 24; John Kieffer/ Getty Images,
pp. 24-25; Storylanding/ Wikipedia, p. 26 (top); Brigitte Merle/ Glow Images, p. 26 (bottom); Kevin
Shields/ Alamy, pp. 26-27; Pakmor, p. 28 (top); Dionisvera, p. 28 (bottom); Stubblefield Photography,
p. 29 (left); B. Speckart, p. 29 (right).

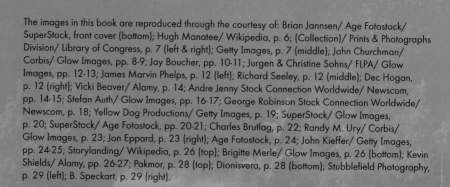